M000106177

Published By
HR Coloring Book Publishing

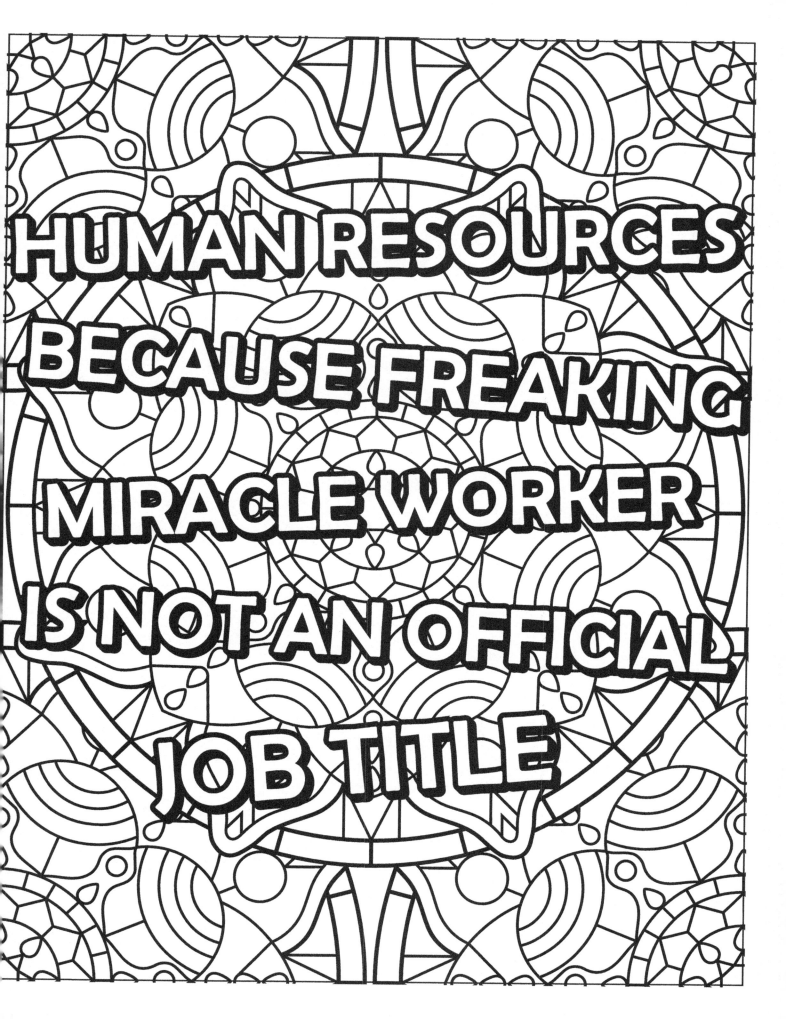

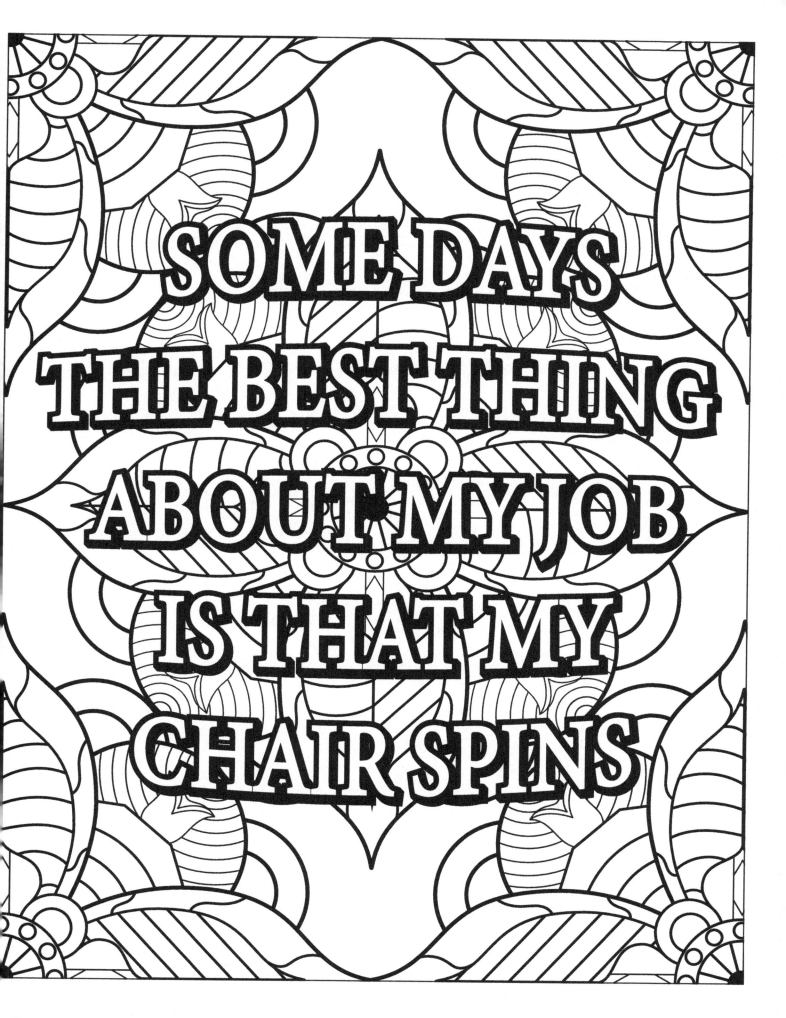

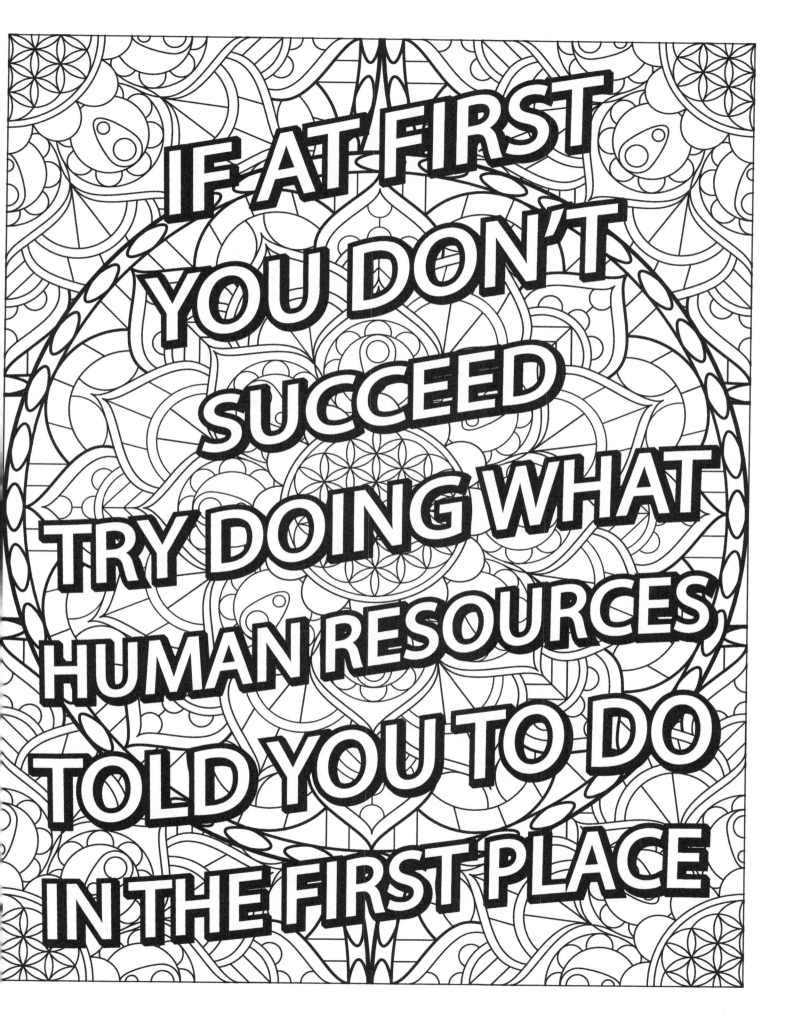

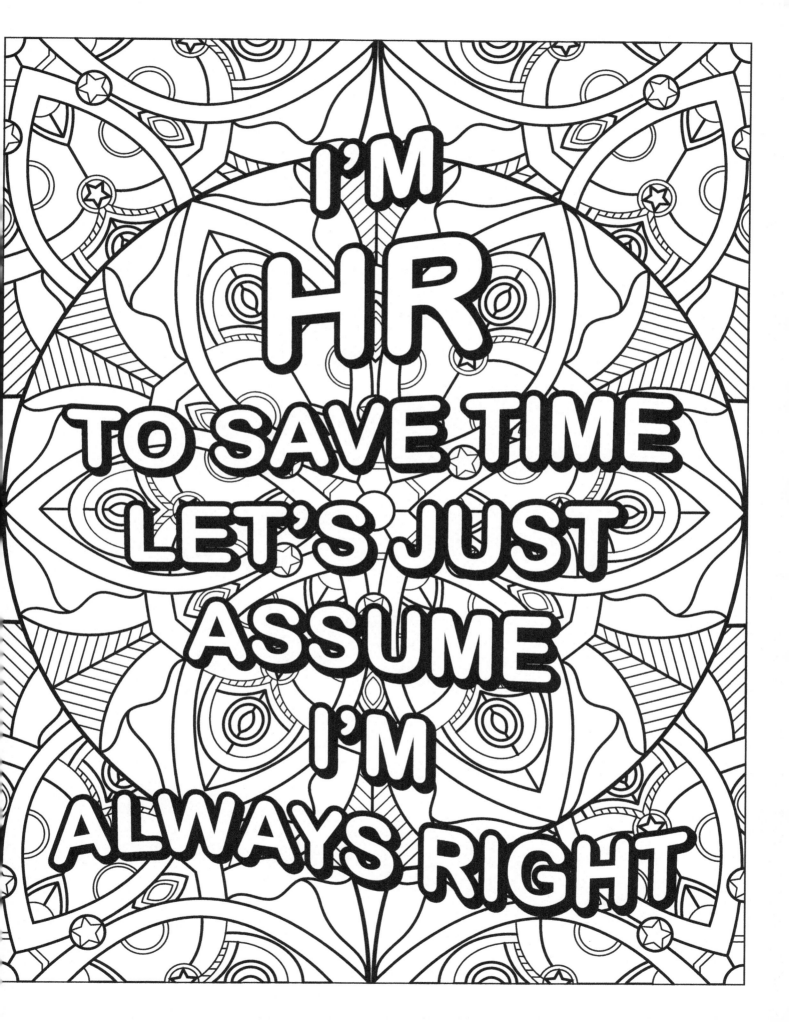

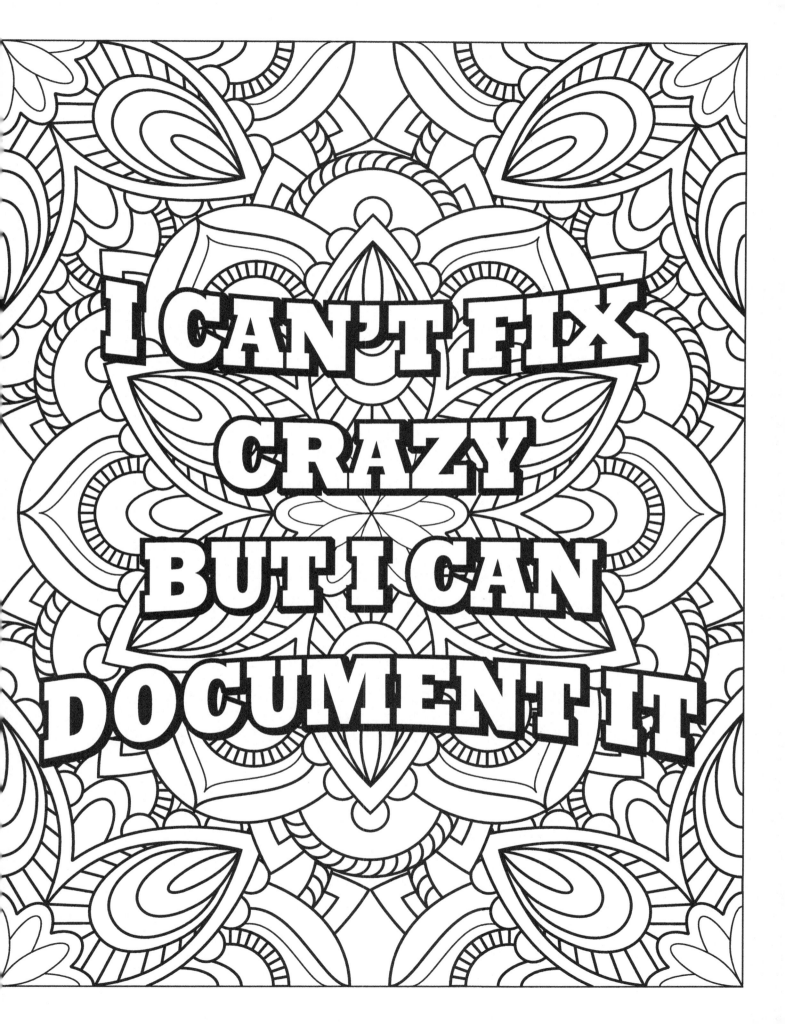

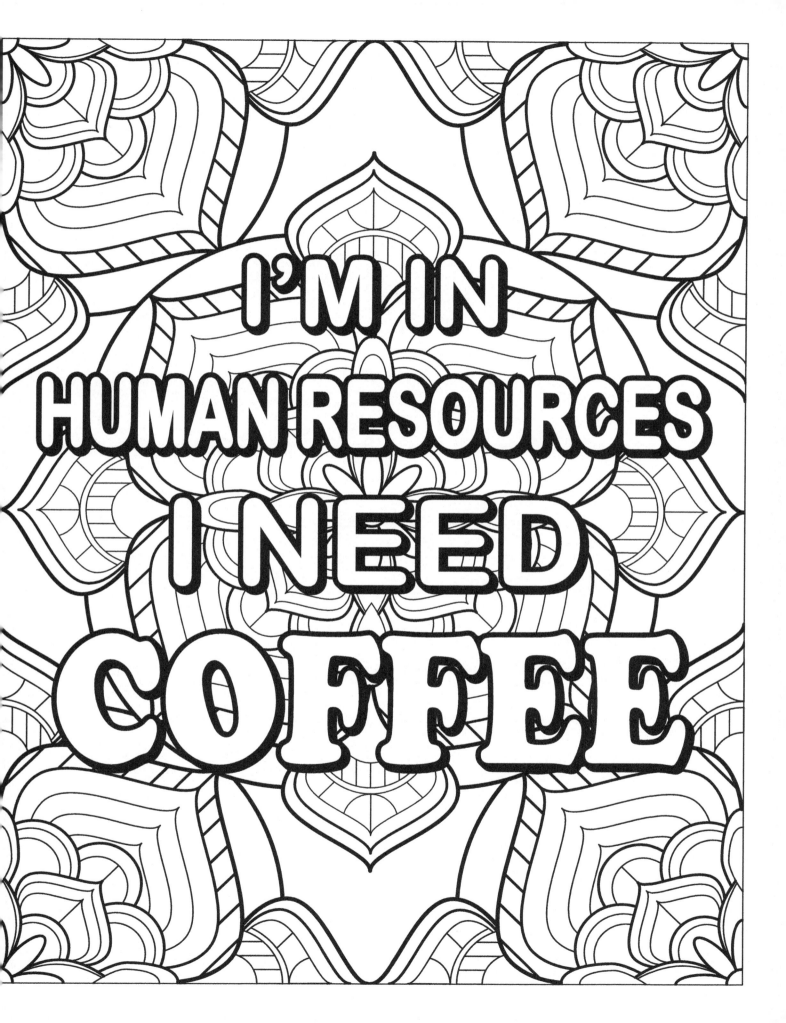

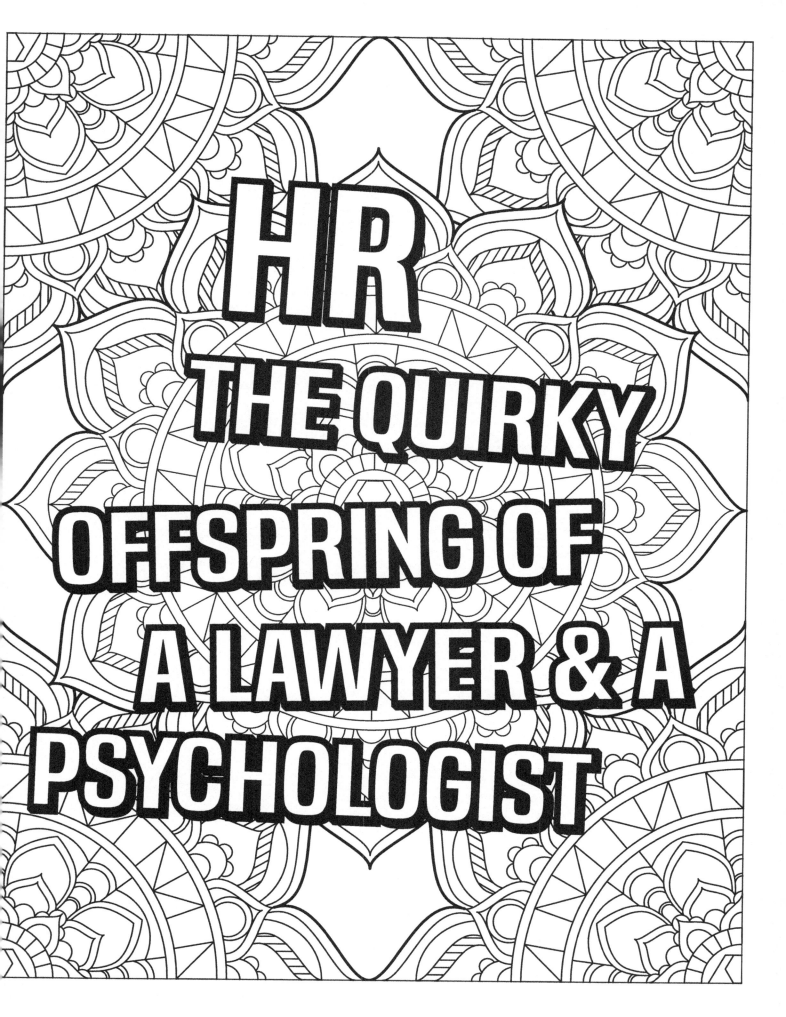

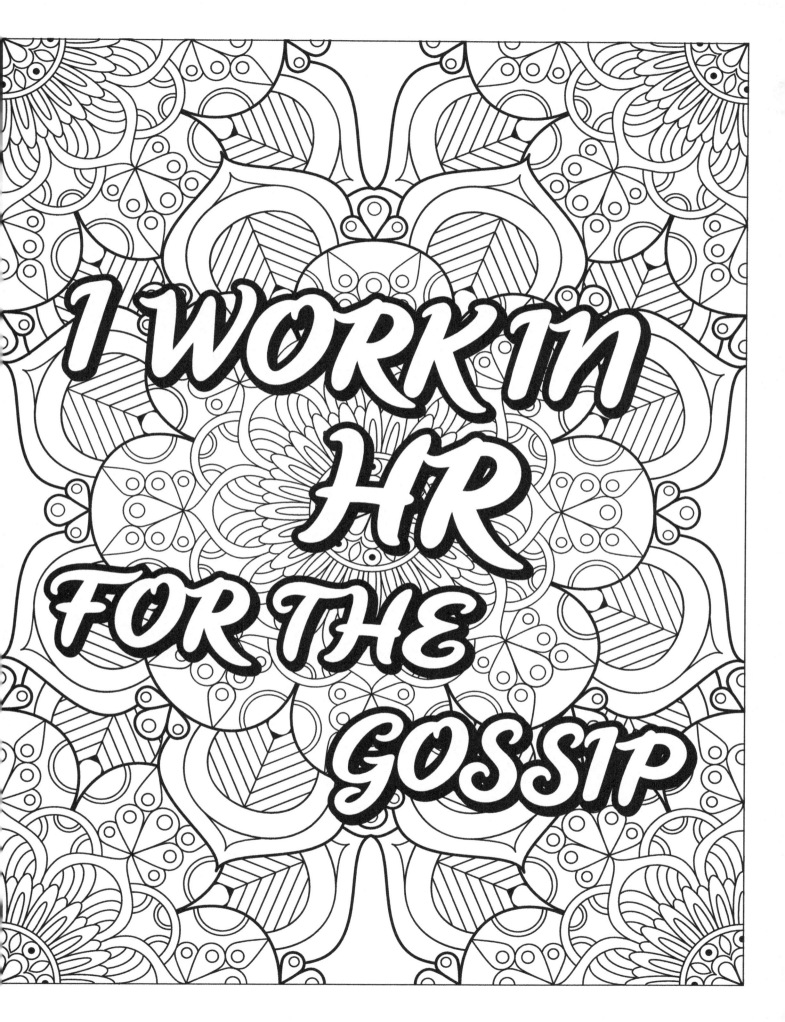

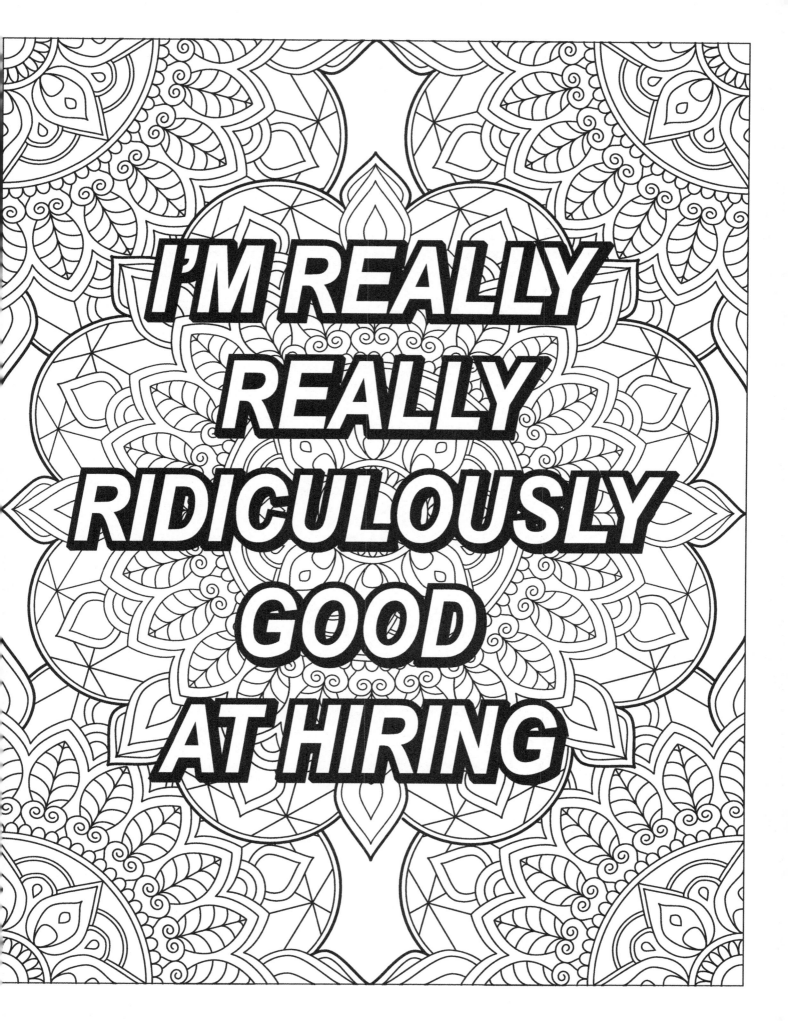

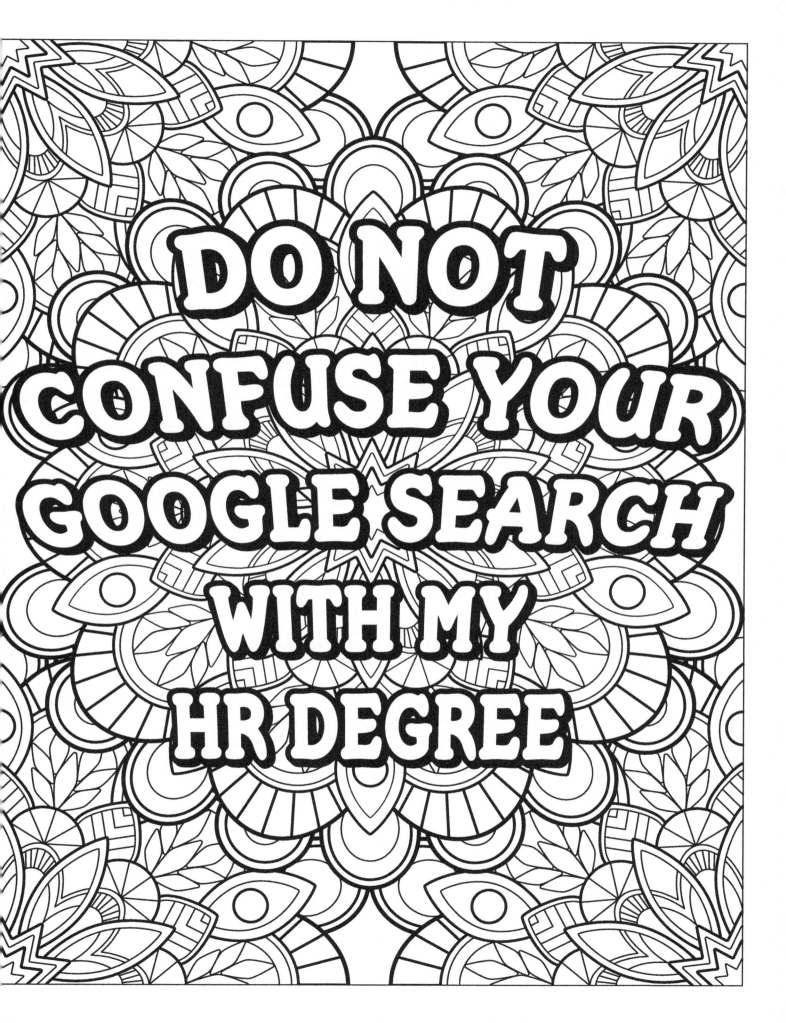

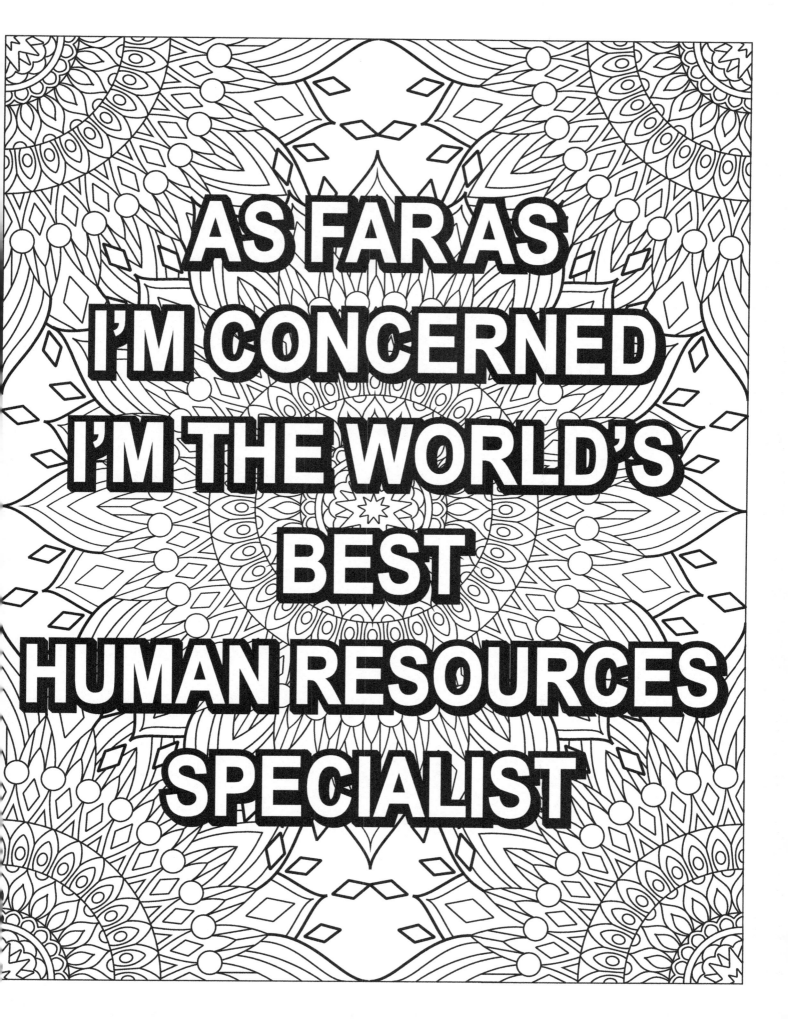

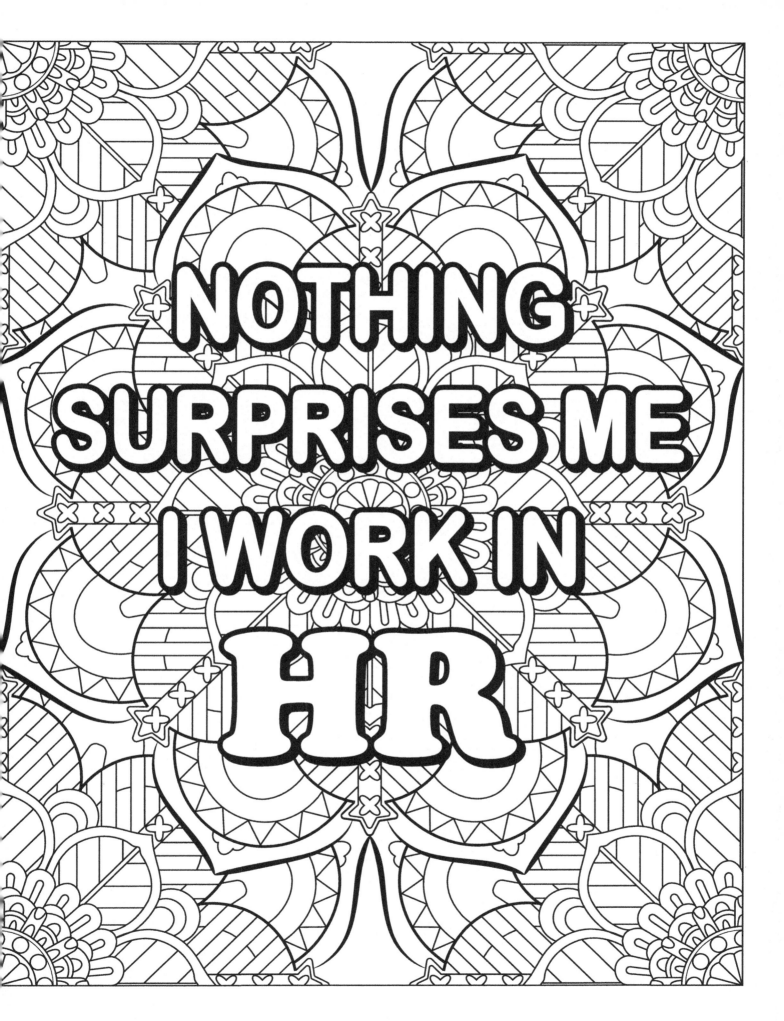

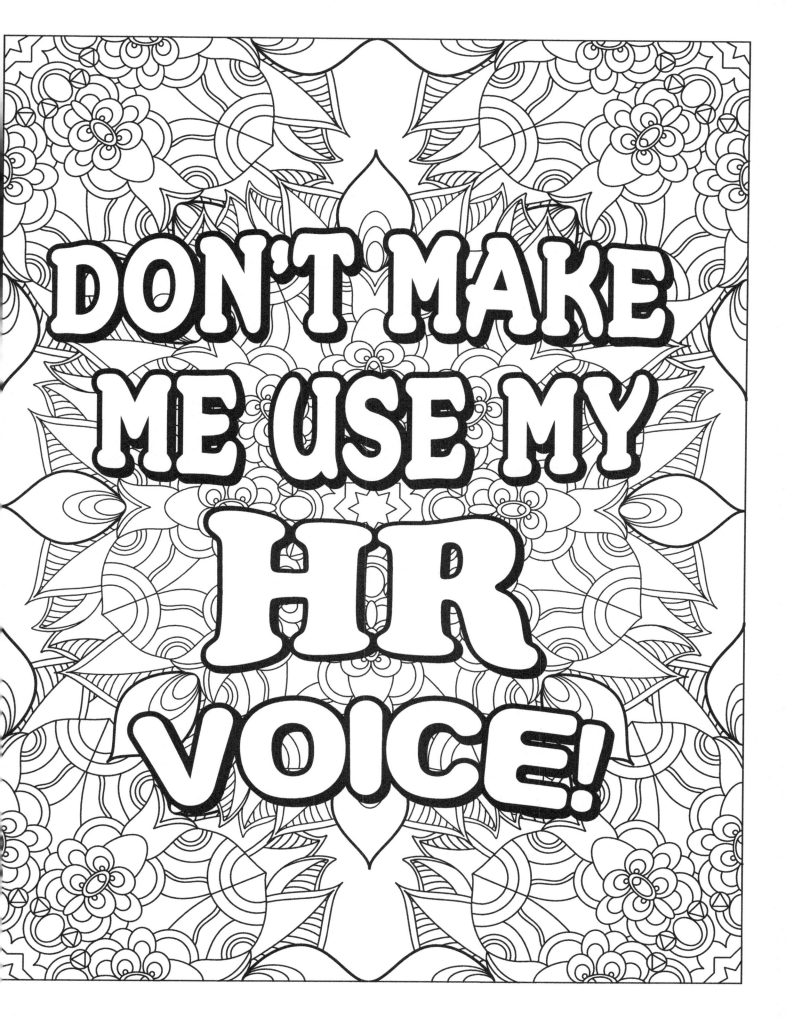

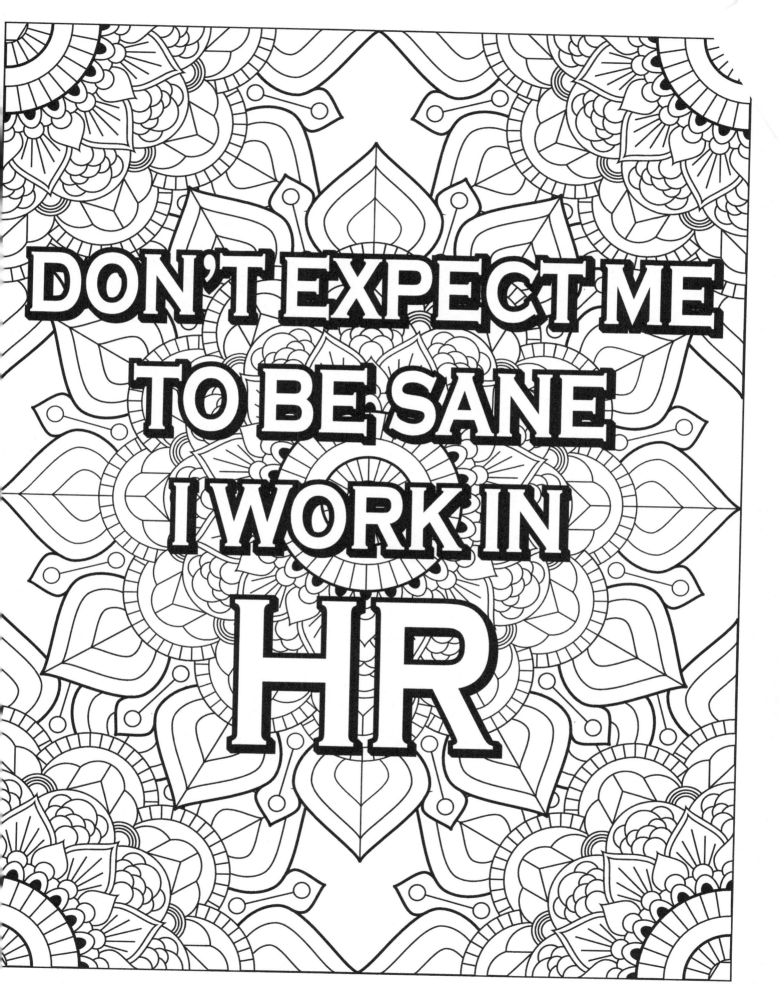

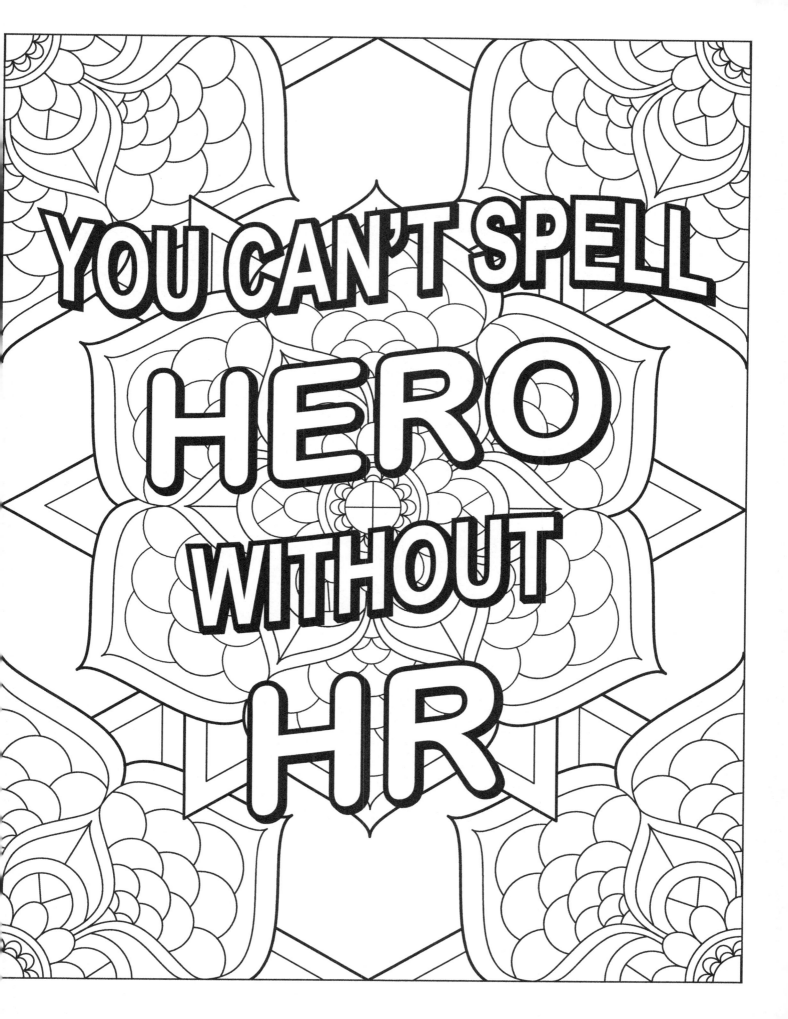

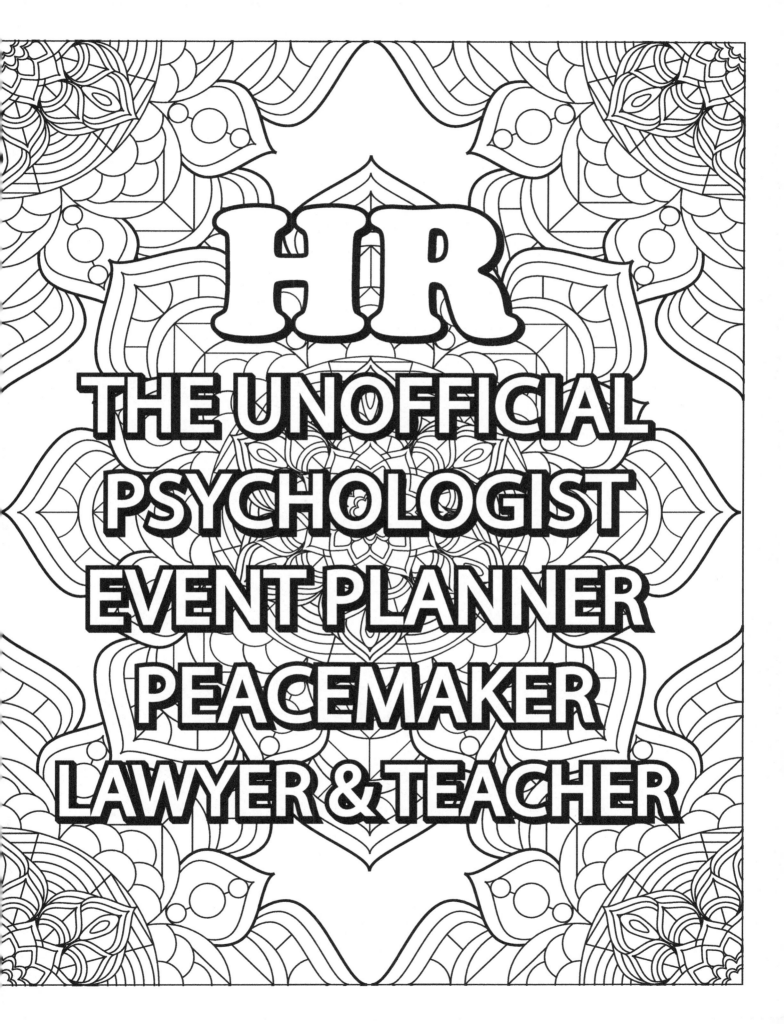

HR

THE UNOFFICIAL
PSYCHOLOGIST
EVENT PLANNER
PEACEMAKER
LAWYER & TEACHER

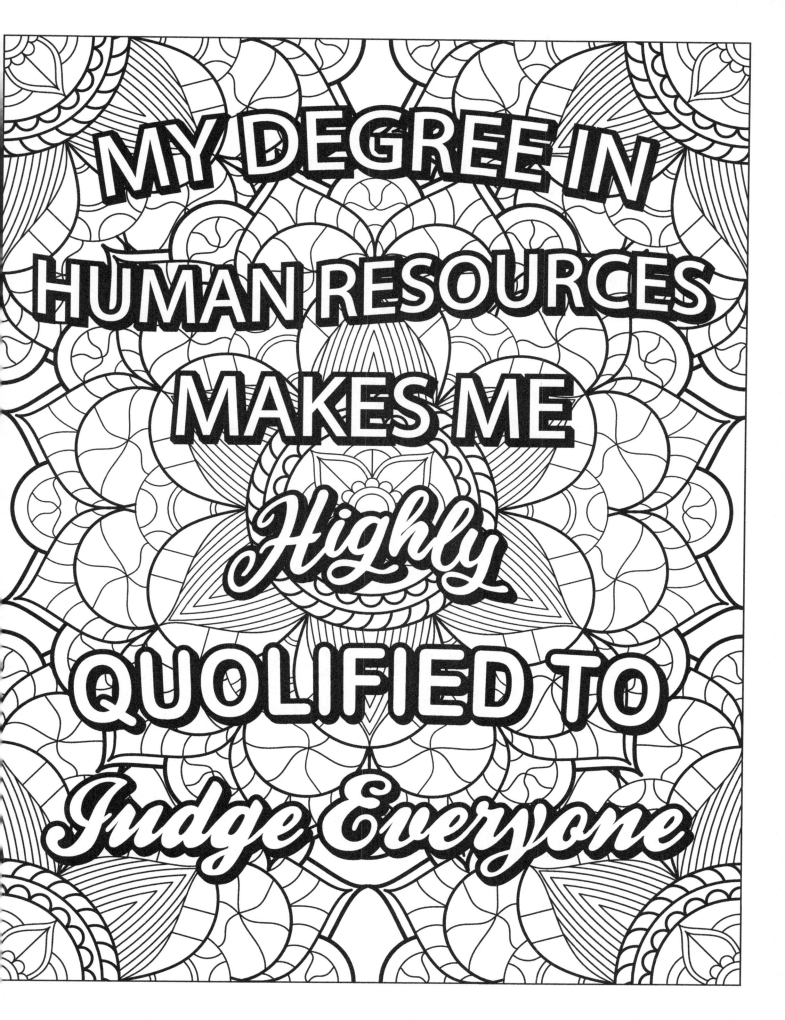

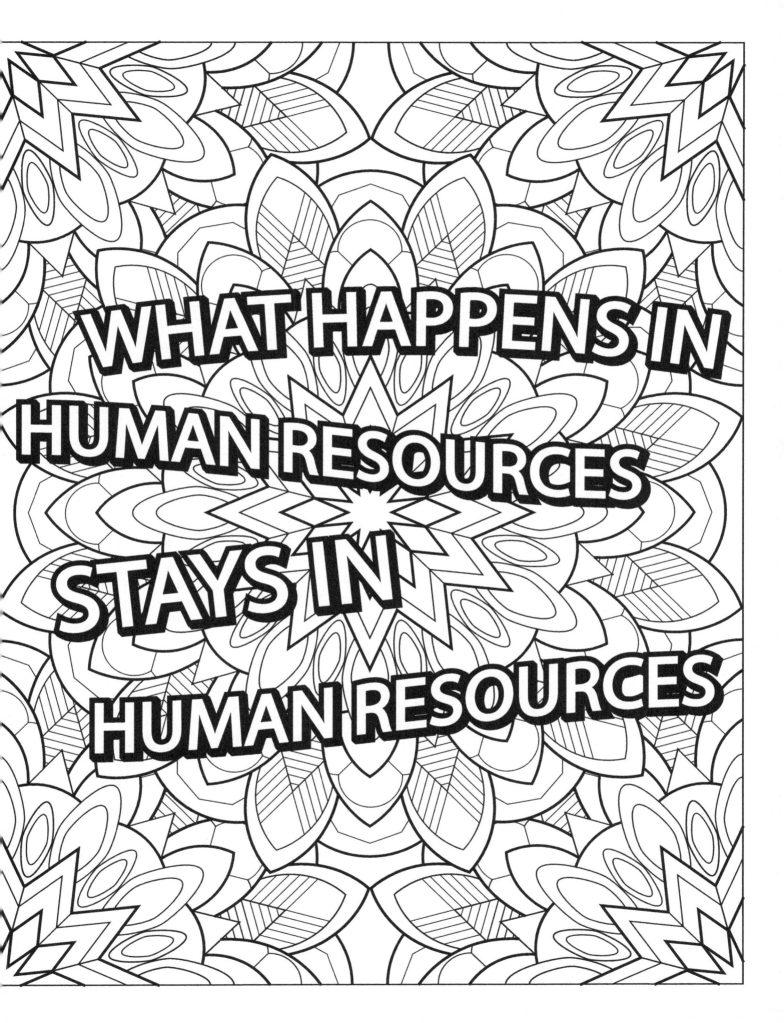

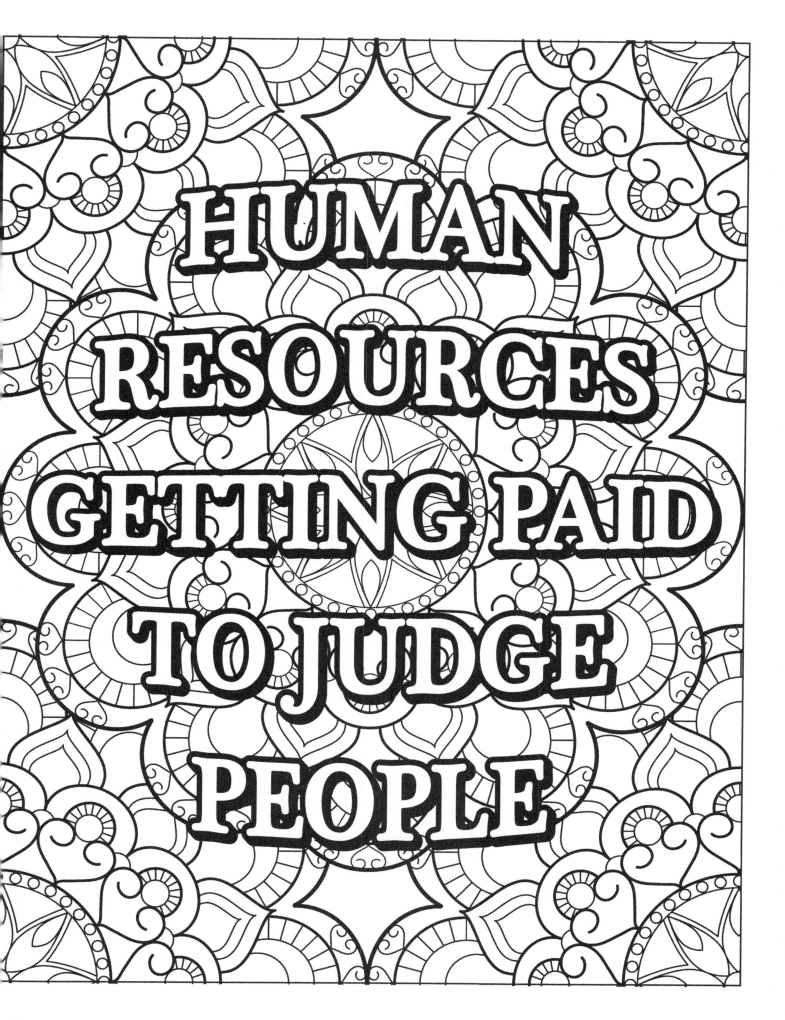

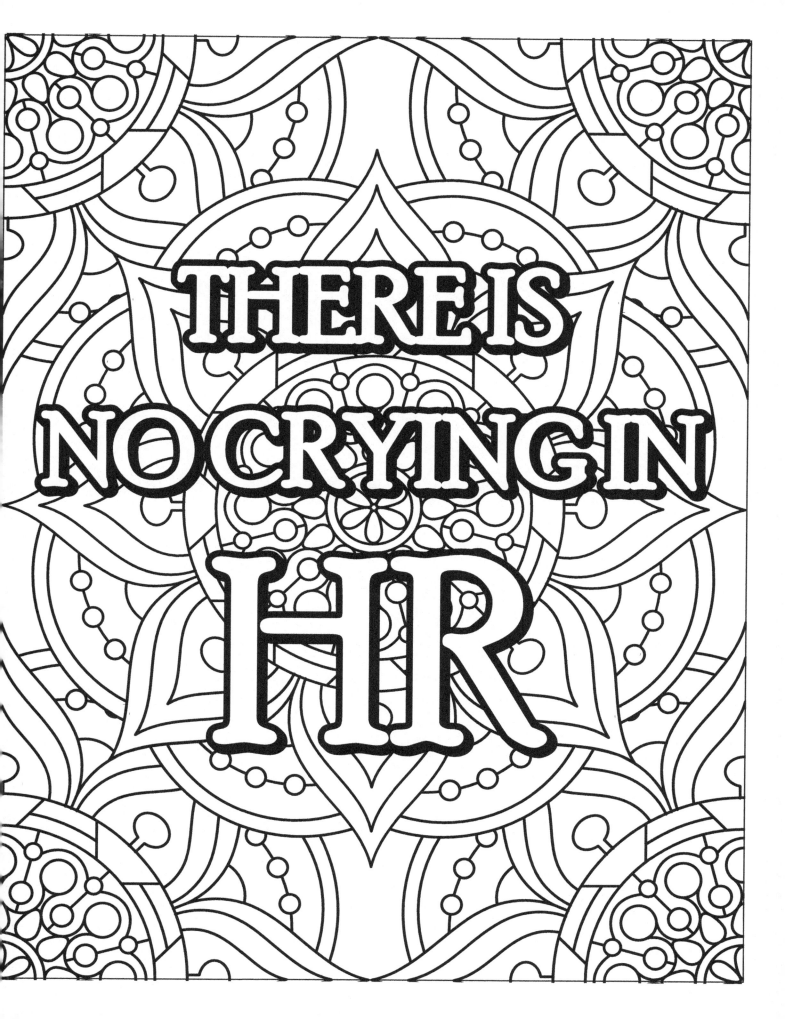

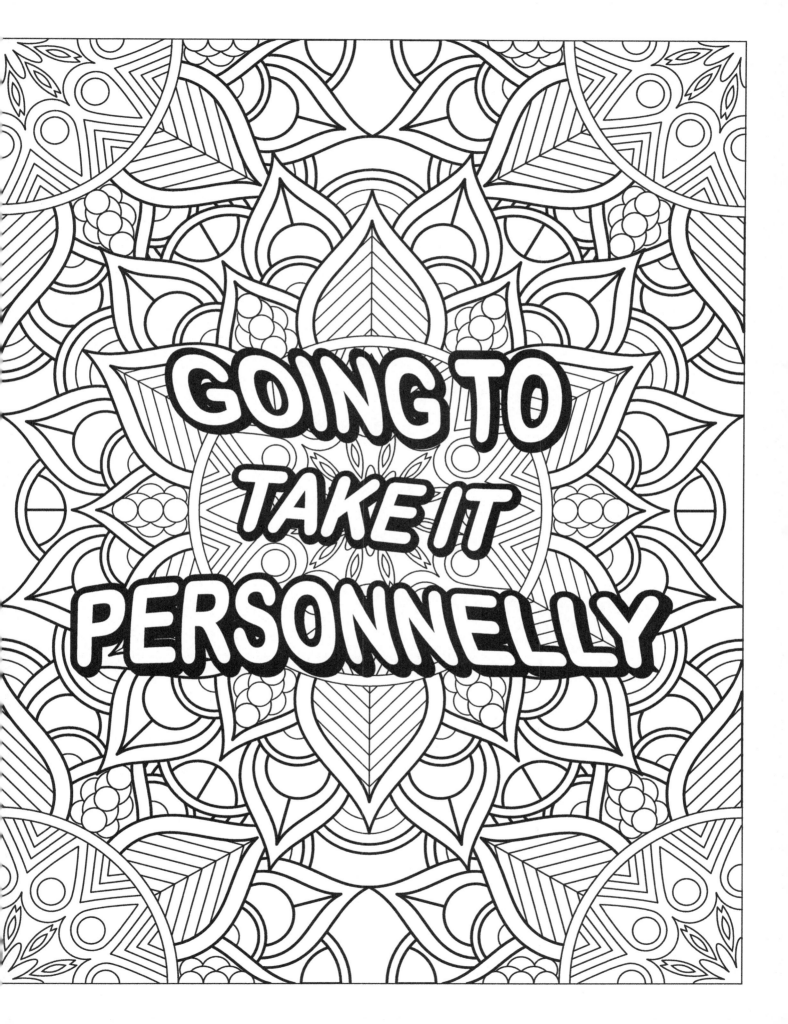

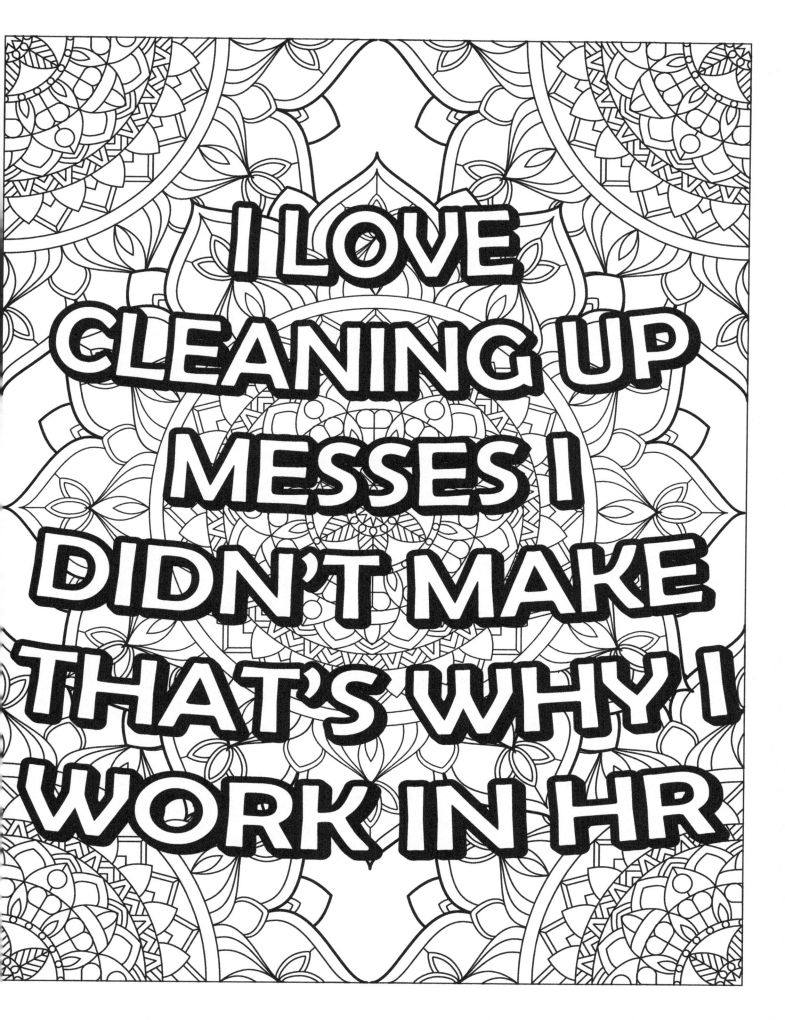

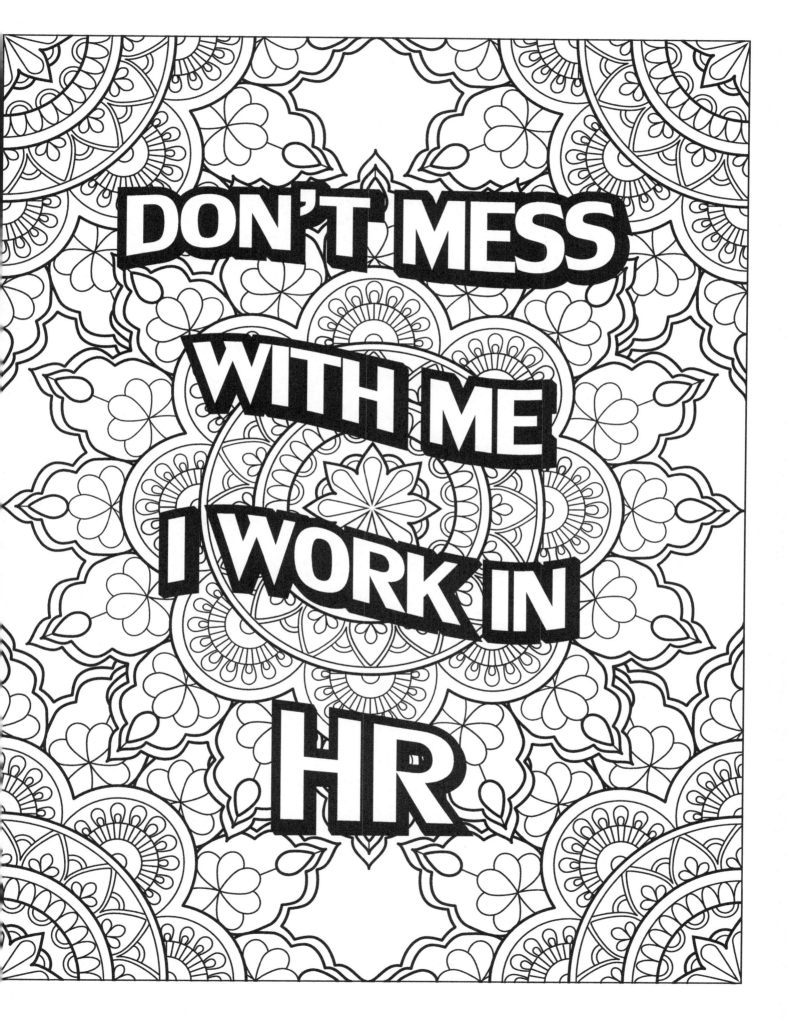

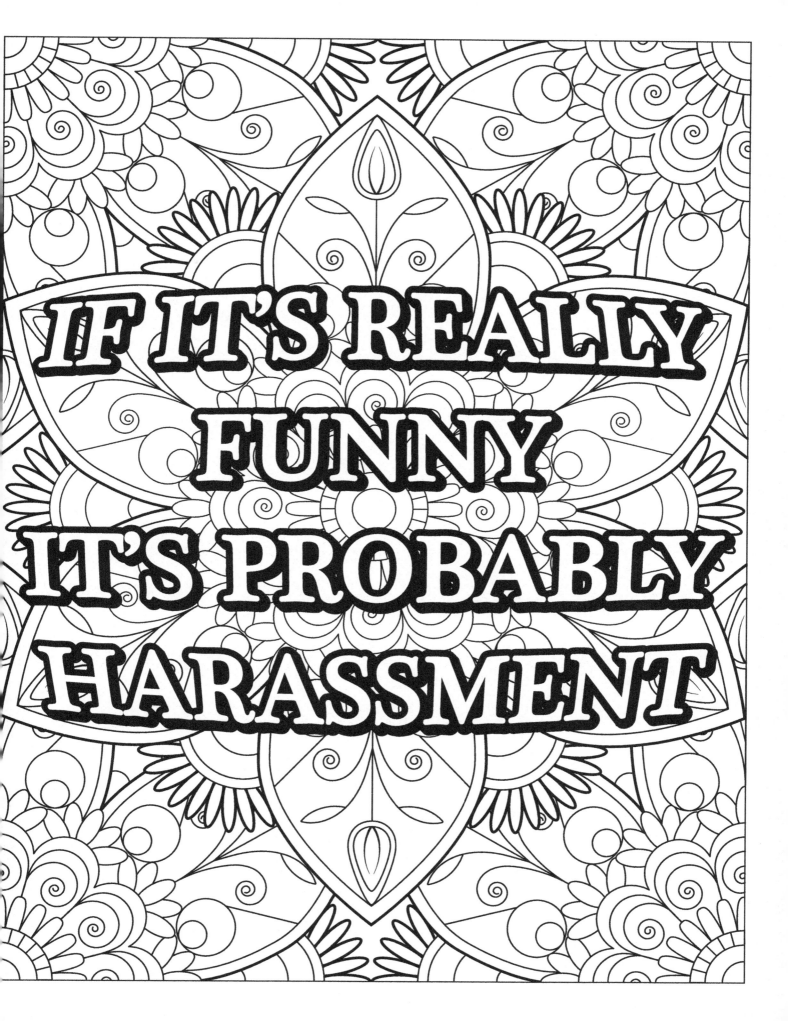

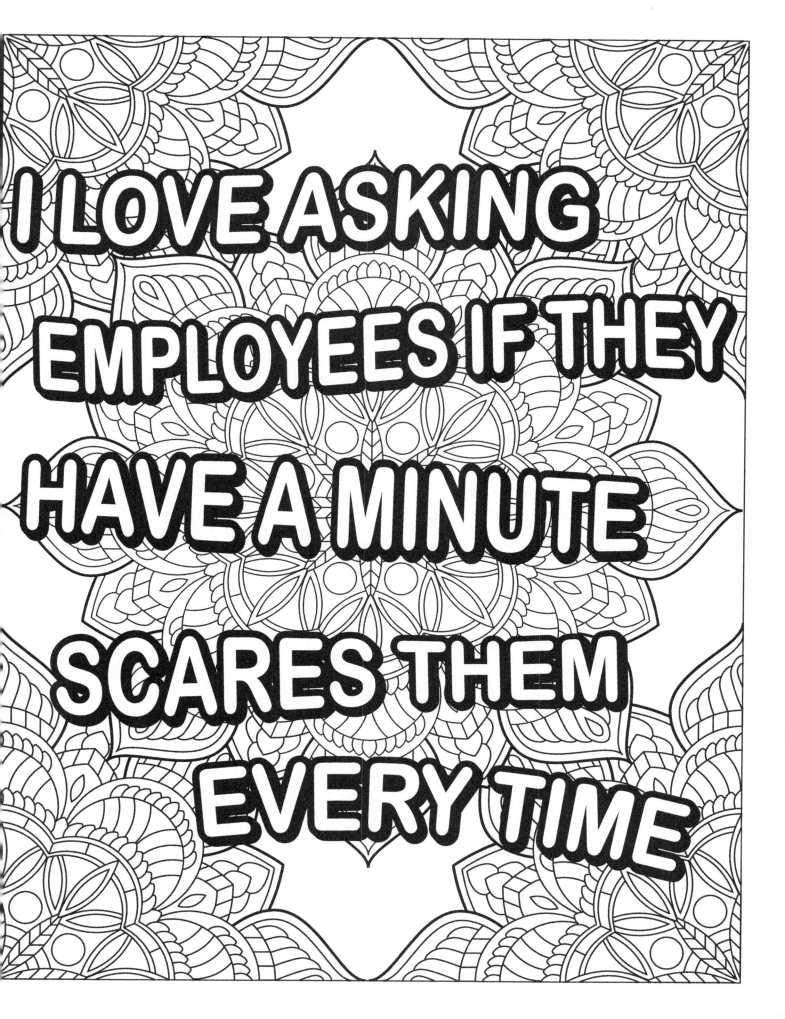

Color Charts Test

Made in the USA
Coppell, TX
15 September 2020

37922609R00031